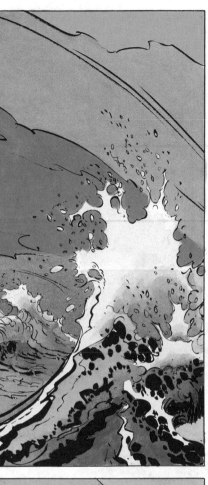

THAT WAS JUST GREAT...

WHAT WAS GREAT!?!

THAT LITTLE MECHANICAL FAILURE, FOLLOWED BY CRASHING THE SHIP IN SO MUCH MUD THE BAY DOORS ARE BLOCKED— AND THE SKIFFS WITH THEM...

A FAILURE... I'M NOT SO SURE.

HERE WAS THING ELSE... SOMETHING LIKE... ER... DARK CLOUD. SED OUT FOR TANT, AND...

AND NOW WE'RE IN THIS CRAP!

IF YOU THINK IT'S EASY!... THIS SORRY EXCUSE FOR A RAFT ISN'T EXACTLY...

PAH!

WATCH IT!

THE CURRENTS ARE STRONG, TOO...

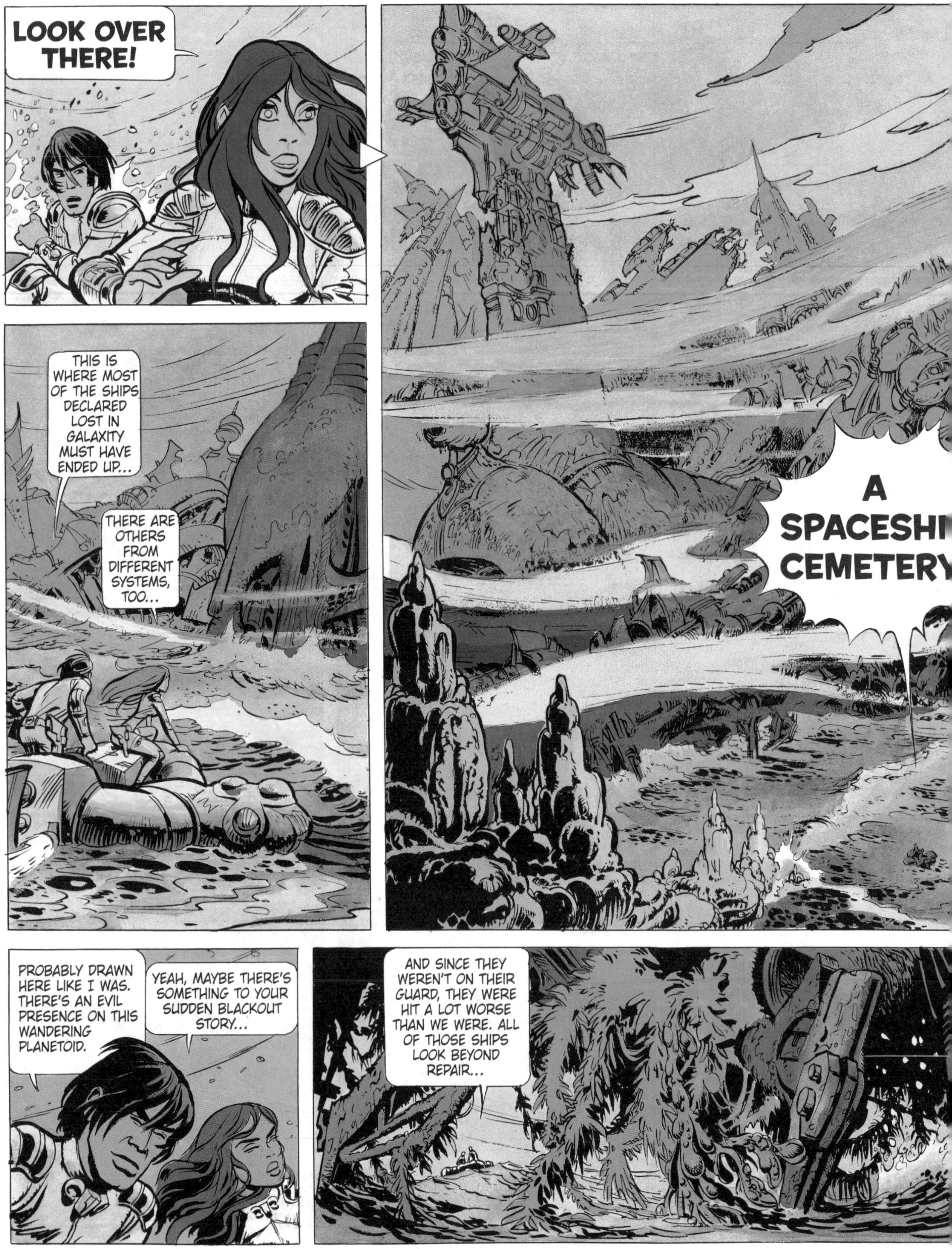
LOOK OVER THERE!
A SPACESHI CEMETERY
THIS IS WHERE MOST OF THE SHIPS DECLARED LOST IN GALAXITY MUST HAVE ENDED UP...
THERE ARE OTHERS FROM DIFFERENT SYSTEMS, TOO...
PROBABLY DRAWN HERE LIKE I WAS. THERE'S AN EVIL PRESENCE ON THIS WANDERING PLANETOID.
YEAH, MAYBE THERE'S SOMETHING TO YOUR SUDDEN BLACKOUT STORY...
AND SINCE THEY WEREN'T ON THEIR GUARD, THEY WERE HIT A LOT WORSE THAN WE WERE. ALL OF THOSE SHIPS LOOK BEYOND REPAIR...

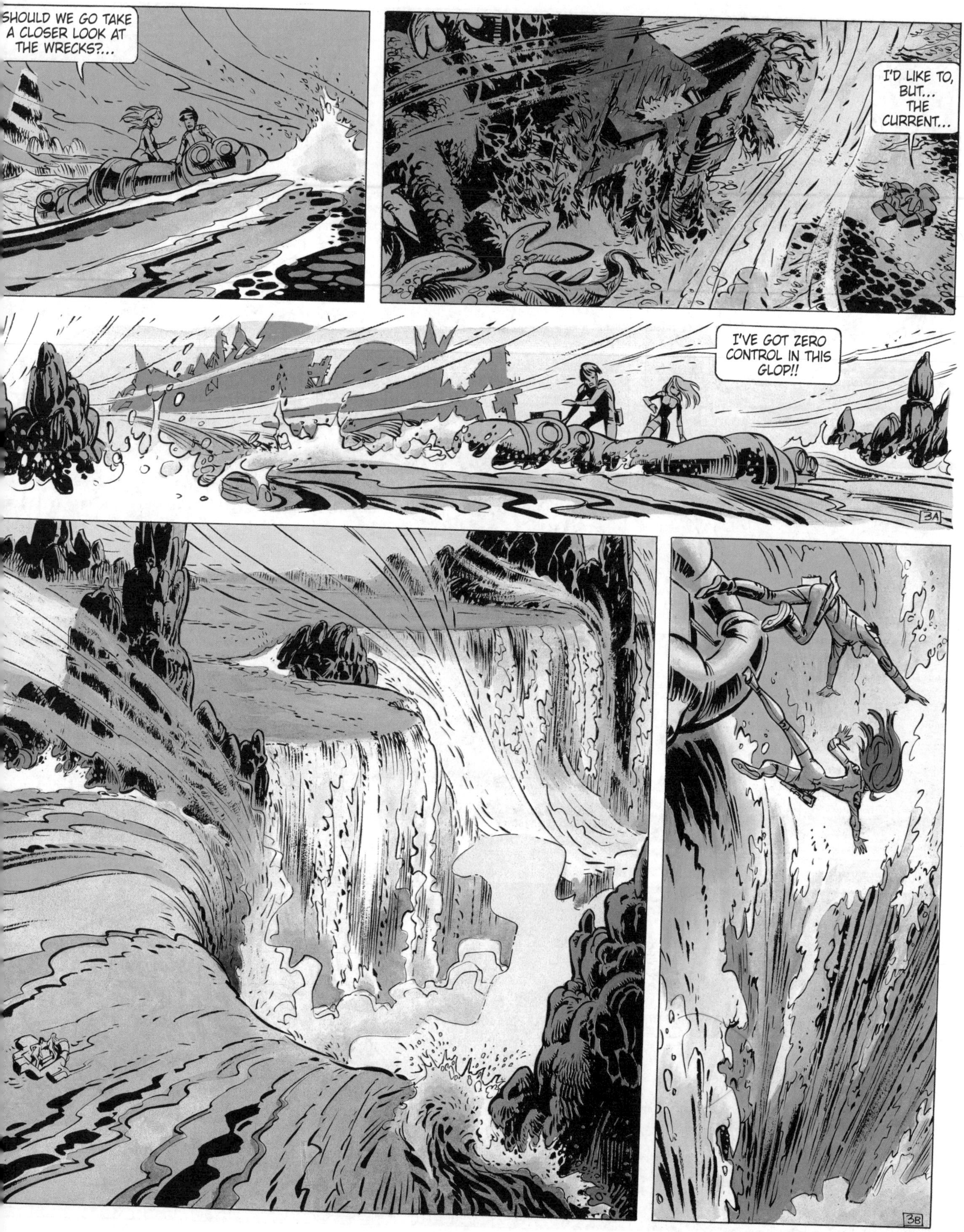
SHOULD WE GO TAKE A CLOSER LOOK AT THE WRECKS?...
I'D LIKE TO, BUT... THE CURRENT...
I'VE GOT ZERO CONTROL IN THIS GLOP!!
3A
3B

IN THE SLUGGISH CHURNING OF THE THICK FLUID...

... DRIFTING FROM EDDY TO EDDY, VALERIAN AND LAURELINE...

... ALREADY UNCONSCIOUS, COME TO REST ON A BANK OF LONG ALGAE...

SUDDENLY, PLUNGING INTO THE NOW-QUIET DEPTHS...

WELL, WAKE THEM UP!

HURRY! THE MASTER IS ALREADY MUCH DISPLEASED... OUR ALGAE HARVEST IS FAR FROM COMPLETE!...

BUT...

LOOK OUT! THEY'RE HERE!!

**THE BIRDS OF MADNESS ARE COMING!!**

THE MASTER MUST HAVE GUIDED YOU HERE SO YOU COULD JOIN HIS SERVICE, LIKE US! SO, GET TO WORK. QUICKLY!

WAIT... THOSE BIRDS OF MADNESS?...

LAURELINE! THAT'S WHAT I SAW WHEN I LOST CONTROL OF THE SHIP!!!

WHAT'S ALL THIS TALK OF A MASTER?... WHAT'S THAT ALL ABOUT!?...

**HEY, YOU TWO!!**

WE'VE FINALLY FOUND A RICH PATCH OF ALGAE. WE MUST WORK HARD TO KEEP THE MASTER'S FURY AT BAY...

ALL RIGHT, ALL RIGHT...

WHAT DO WE DO?

YOU, ALGA... YOU, GRAPPL...

IN THE SILENCE OF BACKBREAKING LABOUR, THE HEAVY VESSEL RAPIDLY FILLS TO THE BRIM WITH A CARGO OF ALGAE...

... WHILE, ABOVE IT, THE BLACK, SILENT THREAT OF THE BIRDS OF MADNESS KEEPS CIRCLING...

HEY, YOU'RE HUMAN... TELL ME...

SHHH! BE SILENT... THE MASTER'S BIRDS... WORK!

?!

AT LAST...

THAT'S ENOUGH! WE'RE GOING BACK TO THE VILLAGE. EVERYONE TO THE WHEELS; WE MUST MAKE UP LOST TIME.

THE BIRDS OF MADNESS ARE LEAVING. THE MASTER IS SATISFIED WITH US...

THE SHIP SAILS AWAY FROM THE CENTRE OF THE LAKE...

VALERIAN! WHAT'S GOING ON? THEY ALL LOOK SO TERRIFIED!

I DON'T UNDERSTAND. OUR PRESENCE DOESN'T SEEM TO SURPRISE THEM, THOUGH...

PFFF... IF YOU WANT MY OPINION, THESE GUYS ARE ALL CRAZY!... WORK FOR THE MASTER AND HIS POULTRY—THAT'S ALL THEY KNOW...

HARVEST ALGAE AND LOTS OF TASTY FOODSTUFFS, WHILE WE EAT ROOTS AND STARVE...

... ALL THAT TO FEED THE MASTER... YOU'VE GOTTA BE NUTS, RIGHT?

LIFE HERE DOESN'T SEEM EASY...

JUST WAIT UNTIL WE'RE BACK THE VILLAGE. YOU'LL SEE—EV THE KIDS ARE STARVING. SO M WORK FOR THAT BASTARD M

H YO

YOU KNOW WHAT'S GOING TO HAPPEN TO YOU! MAYBE IT WAS YOU THE BIRDS OF MADNESS WERE LOOKING FOR EARLIER...

BAH! IF I...

**SILENCE!**
IT'S A MIRACLE THE MASTER'S WRATH HASN'T STRUCK YOUR REBELLIOUS HIDE—AND US WITH IT!!!

THERE'S THE VILLAGE! THE OTHERS ARE BACK ALREADY!

WHAT HARVEST?

WE WERE LUCKY! WE FOUND A RICH SPOT WHILE RESCUING THESE TWO. IF NOT FOR THAT...

GOOD. WE'RE ALMOST DONE HE WE CAN GET UNDERWAY SOON.

YOU, DOWN [N]OW! CHANGE [YOU]R CLOTHES [BE]FORE WE [LEA]VE. HERE [A]RE SOME [WO]RK FROCKS! [YOU] MUST BE [HU]MBLE TO [SE]RVE THE [M]ASTER.

URK! THESE RAGS ARE DISGUSTING!

WORK! WORK! IS THAT THE ONLY WORD THEY KNOW!?

YEP! AND SEE THE RESULT? WE LIVE LIKE ANIMALS... WHEN I THINK ABOUT MY BEAUTIFUL PLANET...

WHERE ARE YOU FROM, KID?

MANADIL, IN THE CYGNUS CONSTELLATION. MY NAME'S SÜL.

MY ACADEMY'S TRAINING SHIP CRASHED HERE NOT TOO LONG AGO. I DON'T PLAN ON ROTTING HERE, THOUGH, LET ME TELL YOU...

WHAT DO YOU MEAN?

[H]EH... YOU'LL SEE! YOU [T]WO DON'T SEEM TO BE [LIK]E THE OTHERS. PIECE OF [AD]VICE, THOUGH... I SAW [YOU]R WEAPONS! KEEP THEM [W]ELL HIDDEN, OR ELSE...

PFFF... SOME MISSIONS ARE ALL ABOUT CHIC, BUT THIS TIME...

SOON, WITH THE LAST PREPARATIONS OVER...

[T]HE FLOTILLA [IS] UNDERWAY...

11

SLOWLY TRAVELLING THROUGH A LAND...

... WHERE SLIMY SWAMPS MAKE WAY...

... FOR A MAZE OF STEEP-SIDED FJORDS...

... AFTER MANY LONG HOURS, THE SHIPS REACH A BARREN COVE.

AND...

FORM THE CARAVAN! **GET MOVING!!**

HURRY, HURRY... THE MASTER IS WAITING...

THIS IS GETTING RIDICULOUS... HOW MUCH LONGER IS THIS GOING TO LAST?!

AS LONG AS TH MASTER HASN'T HIS FILL, THE WH LAND SLAVES AW ONLY THEN CAN SLEEP. BEFORE STARTS ALL OV AGAIN...

ME? OH, YEAH, I AM... BUT I'M HUNGRY, YOU SEE. BESIDES, ON MANADIL WE'RE FREE. SO, LIVING LIKE THIS AIN'T LIVING.

TELL ME, SÜL: THE WAY YOU TALK ABOUT THE MASTER... AREN'T YOU AFRAID OF HIM?

LOOK, THERE'S THE VILLAGE OF FRUITS!

HEY, HERE ARE BIRDS OF MADNESS ABOVE IT!

A NEW CARAVAN, LOADED WITH SCRUMPTIOUS FRUITS, JOINS THE PEOPLE FROM THE LAKE VILLAGE.

YEAH... SOMETHING MUST HAVE HAPPENED AND THE MASTER STRUCK.

LAZINESS... CRWEAK... IS THE DAUGHTER OF WISDOM.

WHAT DID I TELL YOU! ANOTHER ONE THE MASTER DROVE INSANE!

ARE YOU EVER GOING TO EXPLAIN TO US WHO THIS MASTER IS?

THE MASTER!?! HA HA! HA!

COME ON, NOW! NO ONE KNOWS WHO THE MASTER IS! THE ONLY CERTAINTY IS THAT HE CALLS THOSE HE CHOOSES TO HIS SERVICE... AND THAT YOU HAVE TO OBEY HIM....

SOME OF US WERE BORN HERE. OTHERS ARRIVED SO LONG AGO THAT THEY'VE FORGOTTEN ABOUT THEIR PAST LIFE...

YOU KNOW, ON THE MASTER'S LANDS, YOU WALK OR YOU DIE...

WAIT... THAT WOMAN IS EXHAUSTED... WE HAVE TO DO SOMETHING.

WHAT ABOUT HER?

CLOSE RANKS! YOU, THERE, PICK UP THAT WOMAN'S LOAD!

DO AS YOU'RE TOLD! THE MASTER'S LAW PUNISHES THE REBELLIOUS AND THE LAZY! LOOK...

ADVANCING THROUGH A TALL, DAMP-SMELLING FOREST, THE CARAVAN WALKS ON, LEAVING THE CRIPPLED BEHIND...

OH... I MAY BE... SCRITCH... LAZY, BUT I'M ALIVE... CLICK... CAP'N!

LEAVE IT... NOTHING WE CAN DO FOR HER. SHE'LL DIE OF EXHAUSTION. HELP ME INSTEAD...

14

DINED, AS IT PASSES VAST PLAINS, BY
NVOYS OF NEW VILLAGES, HERDING FAT
ALS BEFORE THEM...

... AND FURTHER ON BY THE CARRIERS OF MYSTERIOUS DRINKS, THEIR MOUTHWATERING SMELLS WAFTING.

AT LAST, AFTER MANY EXHAUSTING HOURS OF WALKING...

ARRIVES AT AN
ENSE VALLEY COVERED
TORM CLOUDS AND
LARLY SHAKEN BY
TS OF THUNDER.

SO, THIS IS WHERE THE CITIES OF THE MASTER LIE!

YES! AND THEY SAY IT'S AT THE VERY END, WHERE THE MISTS NEVER LIFT, THAT THE MASTER LIVES...

BUT NO ONE'S EVER GONE TO SEE, HUH?...

SOON THEY ENTER THE FOUL-SMELLING OUTSKIRTS OF THE CITY THE CARAVAN HAS COME TO RESUPPLY.

ALONG NARROW STREETS WHERE CRAFTSMEN WORK TIRELESSLY IN THE SERVICE OF THE MASTER...

... THROUGH DISTRICTS WHERE ARTISTS ARE DECORATING THE STONE WALLS...

... THE NEWCOMERS FINALLY REACH THE CENTRE OF THE CITY.

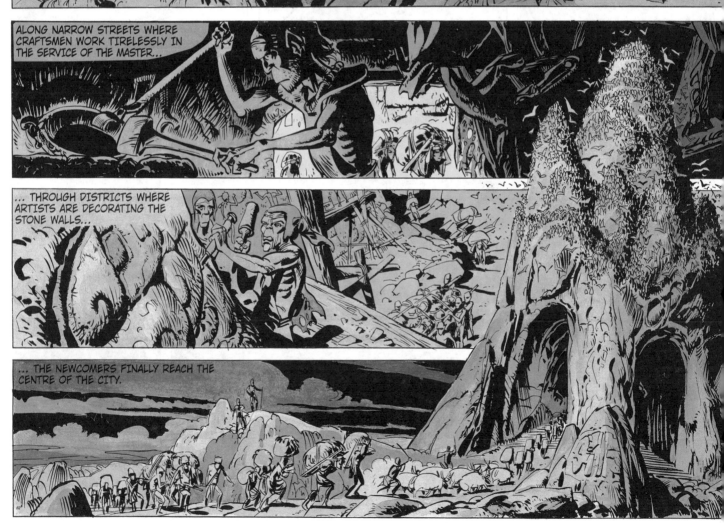

ALL THIS TO PREPARE THE MASTER'S FOOD?

WHAT DO [YOU] THINK, HUH? [WO]RK, WORK, [WO]RK... THIS [IS W]HERE THE [FU]CKING MAGIC [H]APPENS...

[OF] COURSE! BELIEVE [ME I]T'S NO PICNIC TO [ACH]IEVE THE FINAL RESULT!

GREAT! YOU AND YOUR BLASTED HANDS-ON EXPLORATION... I'M BEAT!

OH! WE'RE STILL NOT DONE?...

QUICK! THE BIRDS OF MADNESS ARE HERE! GET TO WORK!

HERE WE GO AGAIN! THAT GUY'S LIKE A BROKEN RECORD!

[TH]E VALERIAN, NAUSEATED BY THE CLOYING SMELL [OF F]OOD, IS SENT TO A SLAUGHTERHOUSE TEAM...

... LAURELINE AND SÜL ARE KEPT BUSY WITH THE CRUSHERS THAT PROCESS THE FRUITS AND ALGAE.

YOU GOING TO FAINT, YOU SISSY? JUST START CUTTING UP THAT SMOOGLOF, AND HURRY UP...

COME ON! COME ON! THE GREAT MEAL IS NEVER LATE!

AT LAST, AMIDST THE LAST-MINUTE BUSTLE...

LET THE MASTER BE SERVED! OPEN THE GATES!!!

17

COME WITH ME! IT'S THE CEREMONY OF THE KLAAR. YOU'VE GOT TO SEE THIS!

... VATS FULL OF SCALDING JUICES, TRANSLUCENT CUPS FILLED TO THE BRIM WITH STRANGE, MULTI-COLOURED DRINKS...

WITH SPECTACULAR POMP, WHERE EVERY GESTURE SEEMS TO HAVE BEEN ARRANGED FOR ALL ETERNITY...

... AROMATIC MEATS, WONDERFULLY DRESSED AND ACCOMPANIED BY DISHES OF SPICE AND FLAGONS OF SAUCE...

... ALTOGETHER, A PRODIGIOUS FEAST MAKES ITS WAY TO THE GREAT BASIN, WATCHED THE STARVING CROWD SLOWLY GATHERING AROUND THE SHRINE.

IT'S DISGUSTIN ALL THIS C PASSING US TO THINK T ALL WE'LL AFTERWARD A SHOT AT LEFTOVERS

18

AND, TO TOP IT OFF, THE BIRDS ARE HERE TO MAKE SURE EVERYTHING GOES SMOOTHLY. DAMNED CRITTERS! I'LL KILL 'EM!

SÜL!

MASTER! THE KLAAR IS READY!

POUR!

YOUR SATISFACTION MAKES YOUR PEOPLE HAPPY!

SUDDENLY, AS THE GLOWING, AROMATIC KLAAR BEGINS TO FLOW...

DOING THAT IN FRONT OF SO MANY STARVING PEOPLE... IT'S JUST WRONG!

SURE IS... ALL THE BETTER TO MAKE US REMEMBER OUR PLACE...

...MAN PEELS OFF FROM THE ...'D AND RUSHES TOWARDS ...BASIN...

... BUT BEFORE HE EVEN REACHES THE TEMPTING, FORBIDDEN MEAL, THE MASTER'S TERRIBLE WINGED MESSENGERS ARE UPON HIM...

THE BIRDS OF MADNESS!

AND ANOTHER ONE DRIVEN INSANE! ENOUGH OF THAT!

SÜL! NO!

BACK, YOU MONSTERS! I'M NOT AFRAID OF YOUR MASTER! I'M NOT!!!

NOT AFRAID!

NOT AFRAID! AAAAH!

THE BIRDS... WHY SO MEAN?...

LITTLE SÜL! IT'S HORRIBLE!!!

LEAVE IT! YOU CAN'T HELP!

OH, NOW YOU SHOW UP! HOW CAN YOU STAND IT?

...DARED ...CH THE ...AR!

THEY GOT WHAT THEY DESERVED...

LOOK AT THE CROWD! THEY LIKE IT! HAVING MARTYRS IS PART OF THE SHOW...

THE BIRDS ARE LEAVING! LOOK!

THANK YOU, MASTER.

NOT AFRAID...

LET THE MASTER'S HUNGER BE SATIATED!

I'M A BIRD, TOO!

THE MASTER IS SATISFIED! LET US NOW HUMBLY THANK HIM FOR ALLOWING US TO SHARE HIS MEAL...

...DREN APPROACH NOW, CARRYING BASKETS ...ED WITH THE MEAGRE LEFTOVERS OF THE ...ER'S FEAST, AND...

NOT AFRAID... I'M NOT... I'LL KILL 'IM, THAT MASTER...

SÜL!

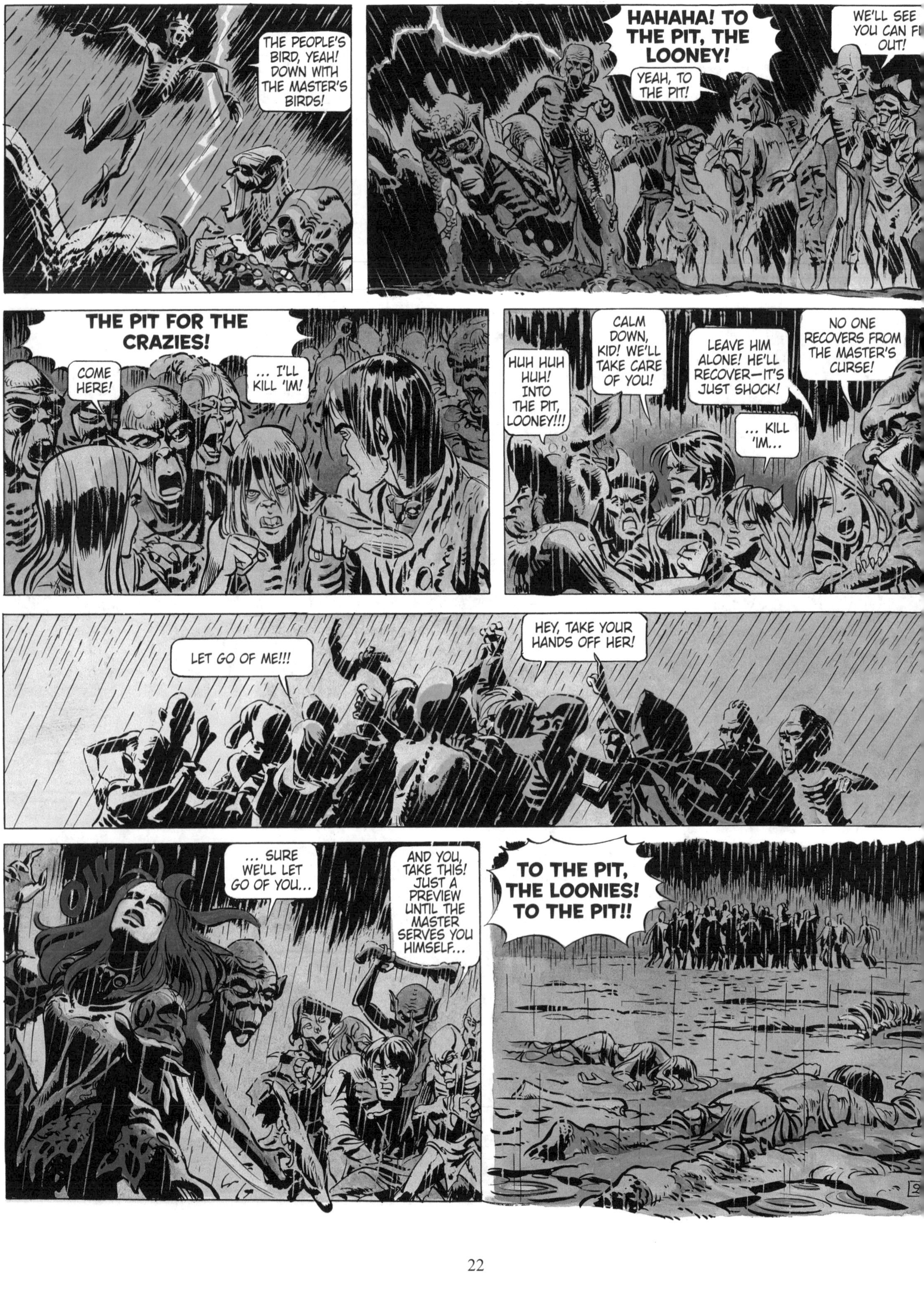
THE PEOPLE'S BIRD, YEAH! DOWN WITH THE MASTER'S BIRDS!
HAHAHA! TO THE PIT, THE LOONEY!
YEAH, TO THE PIT!
WE'LL SEE YOU CAN F OUT!
THE PIT FOR THE CRAZIES!
COME HERE!
... I'LL KILL 'IM!
HUH HUH HUH! INTO THE PIT, LOONEY!!!
CALM DOWN, KID! WE'LL TAKE CARE OF YOU!
LEAVE HIM ALONE! HE'LL RECOVER—IT'S JUST SHOCK!
NO ONE RECOVERS FROM THE MASTER'S CURSE!
... KILL 'IM...
LET GO OF ME!!!
HEY, TAKE YOUR HANDS OFF HER!
OW
... SURE WE'LL LET GO OF YOU...
AND YOU, TAKE THIS! JUST A PREVIEW UNTIL THE MASTER SERVES YOU HIMSELF...
TO THE PIT, THE LOONIES! TO THE PIT!!

YOU ALL RIGHT?

PEACHY... THIS IS SUCH A WONDERFUL MISSION...

IT'S A MAN'S LIFE IN THE SPATIO-TEMPORAL SERVICE, THEY SAID... NO KIDDING... WHERE DID EVERYONE GO?

LOTS OF TRACKS LEADING THAT WAY...

LISTEN TO THE HOWLING!

SO, IS THAT HOW A BIRD OF THE PEOPLE FLIES?!? HA! HA! HA!

AND YOU CAN COOL OFF DOWN THERE!

TOO LATE!

WHERE WAS I? OH, YES... I MAINTAIN THAT THE MASTER ONLY EXISTS BECAUSE... EURG... WE ADMIT HIS EXISTENCE. OTHERWISE...

TSK TSK... THA JUST IDEALISM! EXISTS... FRRR BECAUSE THE PRODUCTION SYS IS SKEWED TO ADVANTAGE...

HEY, THEY DON'T SOUND THAT CRAZY TO ME!

... IT'S ACTUALLY THE FIRST INTELLIGENT THING I'VE HEARD IN A LONG TIME!

I IMAGINE YOU... SHHH... WERE ALSO ON A SURPRISE SPACE CRUISE, YOUNG MAN?

THEN... SCRITCH YOU WON'T MIN SIGNING OUR PETITION? WE'LL IT TO THAT MAS OF THEIRS. W WANT TO PROTE THE TERRIBL ORGANISATION WELCOME. WE'RE FOR SURPRISES EURG... BUT STIL

WHY ARE YOU WORKING SO DARNED HARD?... PSHWICK... THE SEARCH FOR HAPPINESS REQUIRES PRESERVING ONE'S ENERGETIC POTENTIAL, BELIEVE ME...

BACK ON ALDEBARAN, I'M A PROSPECTOR, FIRST CLASS. SO... BLOOK... I'M PROSPECTING. I DON'T GIVE A FIG ABOUT THE MASTER.

I DON'T KNOW IF THEY'RE REALLY CRAZY, BUT...

... WE CAN'T LET THEM ROT DOWN THERE...

HEY, IT'S...

VALERIAN! LAURELINE!!

ET ME OUT OF
RE, OR I'LL HAVE
O GO WHACK
HE MASTER ON
MY OWN!!

YIKES... THAT WAS RASH...

LISTEN TO ME, ALL OF YOU! PLEASE...

IT'S THOSE TWO AGAIN!...

WHY IS THE MASTER SPARING THEM?

THEY'VE JUST ARRIVED! IT WAS OUR CREW WHO RESCUED THEM.

TRY TALKING TO THEM. SOMETIMES IT WORKS...

... WHY LEAVE THOSE POOR SOULS IN THAT
IT? WHY REJECT THEM WHEN THEY'RE SONS
D DAUGHTERS OF SPACE LIKE YOU? WHY BE
FRAID OF THE VILLAINOUS MASTER
HO STARVES YOU? WHEN, ALL
GETHER, UNITED IN COMMON
ENDEAVOUR, YOU COULD
STORE YOUR DIGNITY AND
OVER YOUR FREEDOM!...
HEN PEACE AND LOVE
LD FLOURISH ON THIS
ORLD WHOSE RICHES
ONLY AWAIT...

MAN, HE SUCKS TODAY...

TO THE PIT!

LET'S TEACH THEM A LESSON!

I DON'T THINK YOU REACHED THEM...

AH

OOH BOOH

BOOH

WHAT WOULD THE MASTER BECOME WITHOUT US?

THEY'RE LOONIER THAN THE LOONIES! WHY CHANGE ANYTHING?

GET BACK OR I SHOOT!

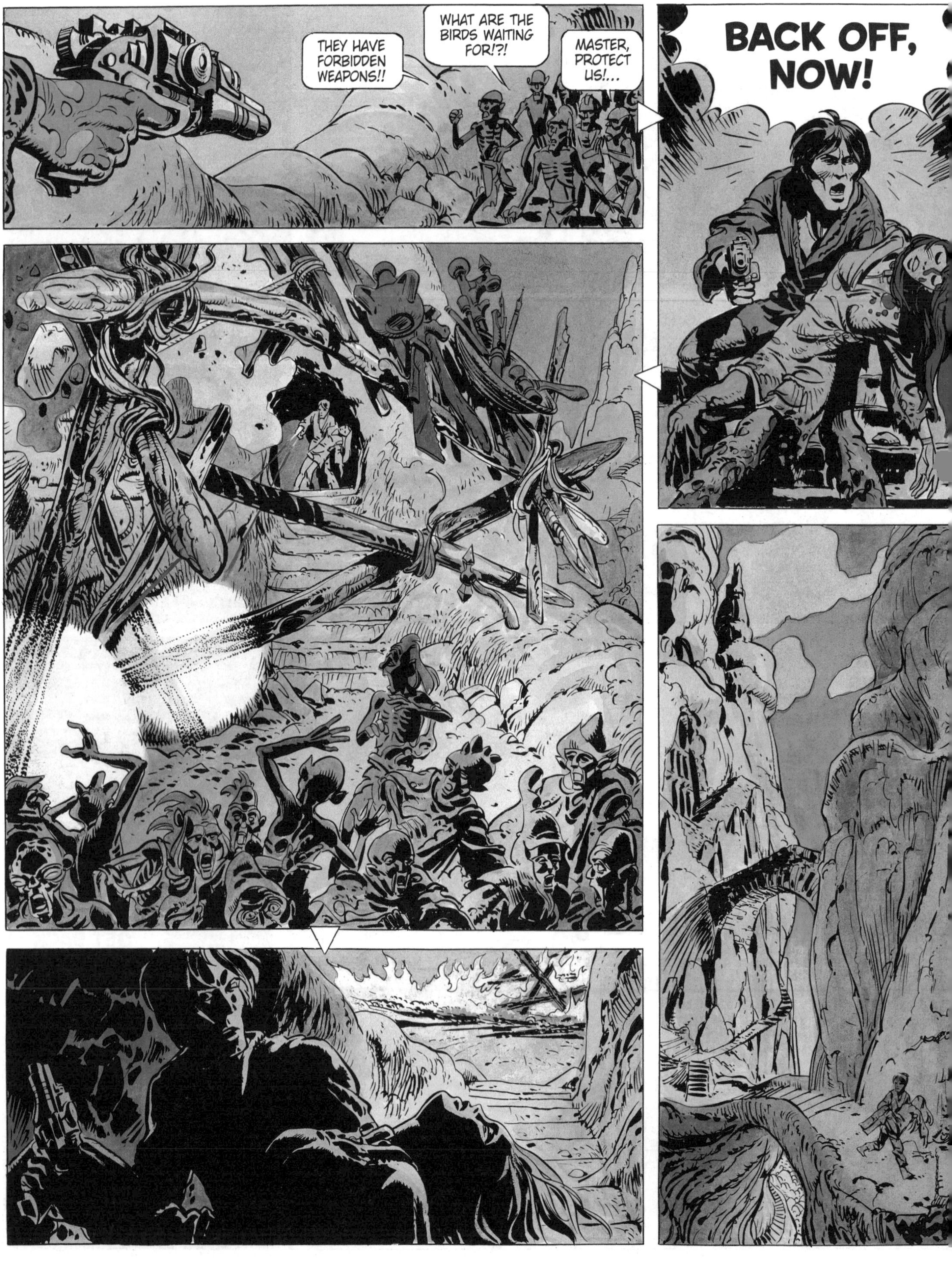
THEY HAVE FORBIDDEN WEAPONS!!
WHAT ARE THE BIRDS WAITING FOR!?!
MASTER, PROTECT US!...
BACK OFF, NOW!

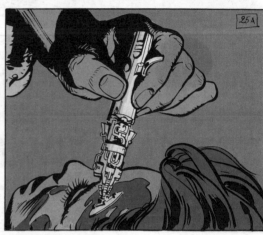

BETTER AND BETTER, BUDDY...

HOW ARE YOU FEELING?

I'VE ALREADY BEEN DROWNED, DRESSED LIKE A HAG, FORCED TO WORK LIKE A SLAVE, KNOCKED OUT AND NOW STONED...

... SO, IF YOU MUST KNOW, I'VE HAD ENOUGH! **ENOUGH!** ENOUGH!!! IF THEY LOVE WORKING FOR THEIR MASTER SO MUCH, LET THEM! I WANT TO GO BACK TO THE SHIP!...

SO THERE!

ERM... WHAT ABOUT SÜL? DO YOU REALLY THINK WE CAN ABANDON HIM?

LOOK! THEY'RE READY TO GO TO SLEEP... TONIGHT THEY CAN REST, BEFORE THE CARAVANS RETURN TO THE MASTER'S RESOURCE-PRODUCING VILLAGES...

HOW ABOUT WE TRY AND GET THE KID OUT ONCE THEY'RE ASLEEP, HMM? AFTER THAT, I PROMISE, WE CAN GO...

A LITTLE LATER...

ALL RIGHT, EVERY-ONE'S OUT...

SO ARE THEY, DON'T YOU THINK?

JUST AS WELL...

28

... BECAUSE...

... I'D RATHER WE...

... DIDN'T MAKE TOO MUCH NOISE...

PLOTCH

BRAOU

SPLAT

YOU! HEY, I... CRWEAK... KNEW THAT I COULD COUNT ON YOU TO GO... CLACK... WHACK THE MASTER. AIN'T IT SO?

AIN'T IT? AIN'T IT? I AIN'T AFRAID, YOU KNOW... CRITCH... WE'RE ALL GOING TO ATTACK HIM...

OF COURSE WE'RE GOING, SÜL, LITTLE BUDDY, BUT FIRST...

ATTACK THE MASTER? IF YOU'RE COUNTING ON US...

... YOU'D BETTER... PLICK... HURRY THINGS UP, YOUNG MAN. BECAUSE...

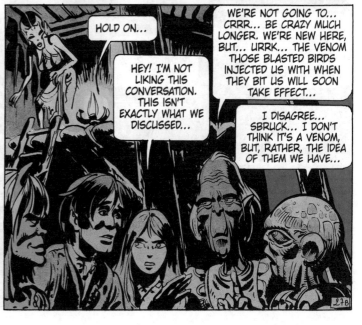

HOLD ON...

HEY! I'M NOT LIKING THIS CONVERSATION. THIS ISN'T EXACTLY WHAT WE DISCUSSED...

WE'RE NOT GOING TO... CRRR... BE CRAZY MUCH LONGER. WE'RE NEW HERE, BUT... URRK... THE VENOM THOSE BLASTED BIRDS INJECTED US WITH WHEN THEY BIT US WILL SOON TAKE EFFECT...

I DISAGREE... SBRUCK... I DON'T THINK IT'S A VENOM, BUT, RATHER, THE IDEA OF THEM WE HAVE...

29

I SAY!... BRRR... I RECOGNISE YOU! YOU WERE ONE OF THE ORGANISERS OF OUR SURPRISE CRUISE...

I CERTAINLY HOPE... BLUCK... THAT YOU'RE GOING TO TAKE US TO SEE THAT MASTER CHARACTER AND THAT... PLOOTCH... THE STANDARD OF ACCOMMODATION WILL IMPROVE...

WE'LL DISCUSS IT LATER...

COME NOW, MY FRIEND!... BINK... ALL THOSE POOR SERVANTS OF THE MASTER YOU SAW UP THERE WERE BITTEN IN THEIR TIME. THAT IS WHY THEY ARE SO DOCILE.

NONSENSE... SCRITCH... YOU KNOW FULL WE THAT MOST OF THE OBEY... PLOCK... OUT SHEER CONFORMIT

WAHHHH... WHAT'S GOING ON? I... BRRRRR... WAS SLEEPING!

WHAT'S ALL THIS HULLABALOO? OBEYIN PLUTCH... THE MAST OR OBEYING SOMEO ELSE... WHAT MATTER PROSPECTING.

YOU WERE MUCH MORE ELEGANT... BLLBLL... THE LAST TIME I SAW YOU IN THE OFFICES OF...

A REFUND!... CRACK... THAT'S WHAT IT'LL COST YOU IF OUR PETITION ISN'T ACCEPTED!

WHAT'S CERTAIN... PROTCH... IS THAT THE BIRDS OF MADNESS ARE GOING TO MAKE US LIKE THE OTHER WORKERS...

NOT AT ALL!... PLOP... NO ONE IS LIKE ANYONE ELSE ON THIS PLANETOID.

WHAT I WANT IS PROPER TERRAIN, SEE, NOT LIKE... SCRITCH... THIS MUDHOLE HERE...

ERM... I DON'T WANT TO RUSH ANYONE, BUT...

DUDES ARE GONNA DAMAGE THEIR BRAINS... SPLURRR... THINKING SO MUCH! IT AIN'T GOOD SO SOON AFTER WAKING UP...

AGAINST THE MASTER... SHHHHH... THE PEOPLE'S BIRD WILL TAKE FLIGHT!!

... THE ESCAPE'S THIS WAY!

ESCAPE? WHAT ESCAPE?

THAT'S TRUE, ACTUALLY. MAYBE WE COULD STAY HERE. HERE IS FUN. WE'RE LEARNING A LOT OF AMUSING THINGS HERE...

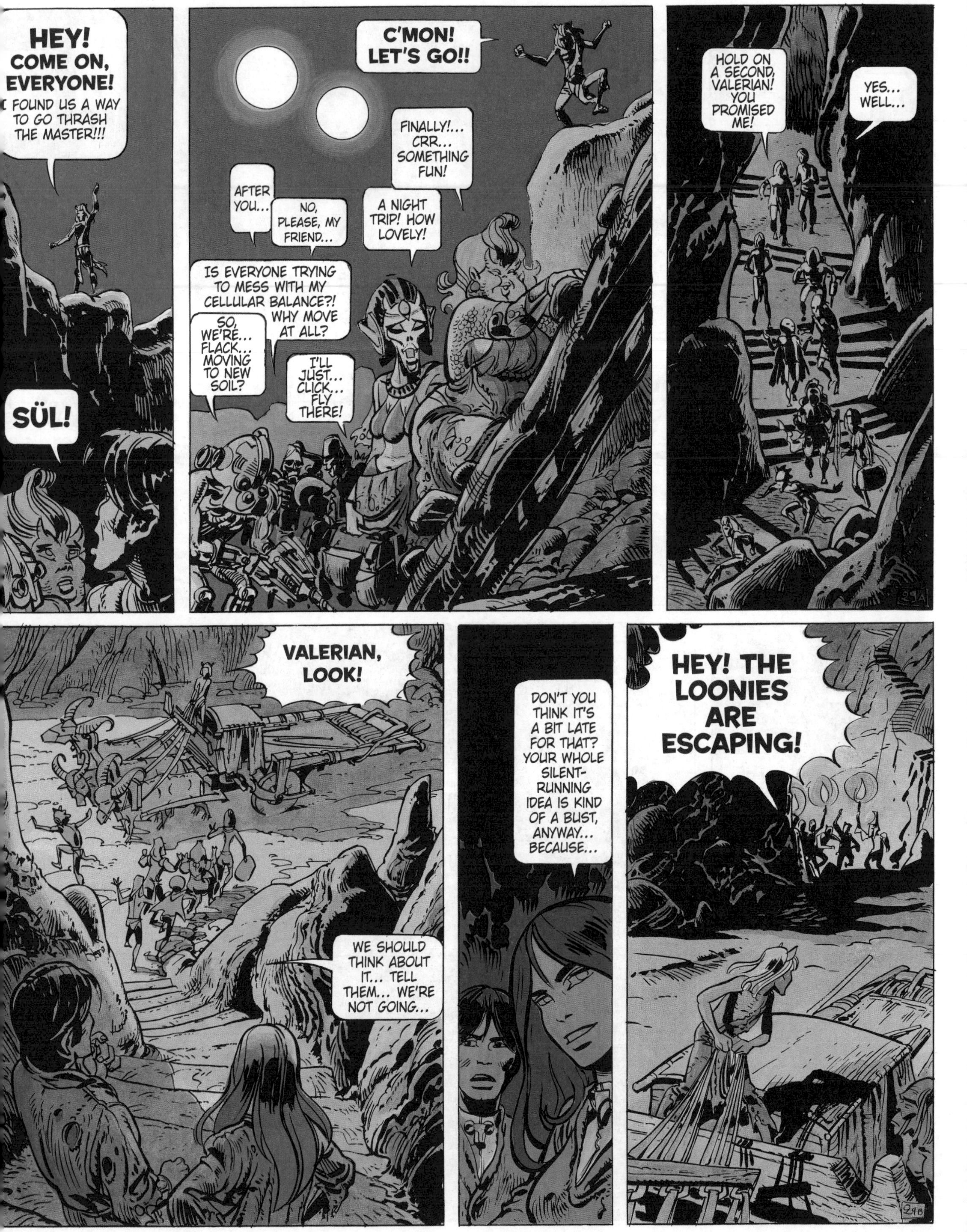

HEY! COME ON, EVERYONE! I FOUND US A WAY TO GO THRASH THE MASTER!!!
SÜL!
C'MON! LET'S GO!!
FINALLY!... CRR... SOMETHING FUN!
AFTER YOU...
NO, PLEASE, MY FRIEND...
A NIGHT TRIP! HOW LOVELY!
IS EVERYONE TRYING TO MESS WITH MY CELLULAR BALANCE?! WHY MOVE AT ALL?
SO, WE'RE... FLACK... MOVING TO NEW SOIL?
I'LL JUST... CLICK... FLY THERE!
HOLD ON A SECOND, VALERIAN! YOU PROMISED ME!
YES... WELL...
VALERIAN, LOOK!
WE SHOULD THINK ABOUT IT... TELL THEM... WE'RE NOT GOING...
DON'T YOU THINK IT'S A BIT LATE FOR THAT? YOUR WHOLE SILENT-RUNNING IDEA IS KIND OF A BUST, ANYWAY... BECAUSE...
HEY! THE LOONIES ARE ESCAPING!

HALT!

GET THE CHARIOTS!

YAAAA

DID YOU... CRRR... BRING OUR WARDROBE?

YES!... DEAR ME... THESE SEATS ARE SO UNCOMFORTABLE!

COME ON, HOP IN! NO CHOICE!

NO NE TO PUS GET I

WHAT ABOUT HIM? HE CAN'T... BLURK... REALLY FLY, YOU KNOW...

OH... SLUC THAT REMA TO BE SEE IF HE REA WANTS IT, M HE WILL...

YEAH, WELL, JUST IN CASE... COME HERE, YOU!

THE PEOPLE'S BIRD IS FLYING!

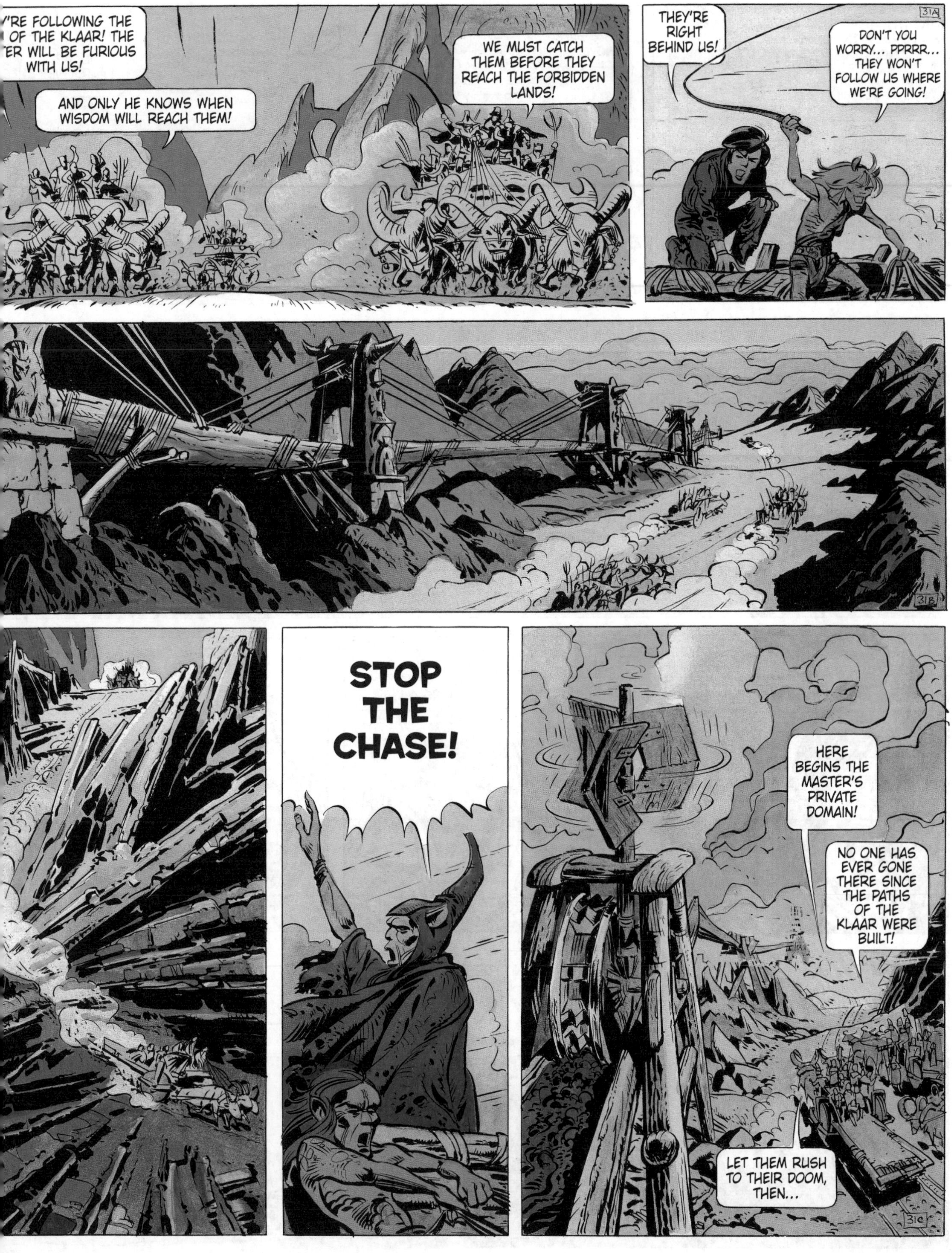
'RE FOLLOWING THE OF THE KLAAR! THE ER WILL BE FURIOUS WITH US!
AND ONLY HE KNOWS WHEN WISDOM WILL REACH THEM!
WE MUST CATCH THEM BEFORE THEY REACH THE FORBIDDEN LANDS!
THEY'RE RIGHT BEHIND US!
DON'T YOU WORRY... PPRRR... THEY WON'T FOLLOW US WHERE WE'RE GOING!
STOP THE CHASE!
HERE BEGINS THE MASTER'S PRIVATE DOMAIN!
NO ONE HAS EVER GONE THERE SINCE THE PATHS OF THE KLAAR WERE BUILT!
LET THEM RUSH TO THEIR DOOM, THEN...

AS THE HEAVY CHARIOT PUSHES DEEPER INTO THE MISTS THAT FOREVER COVER THE FORBIDDEN LANDS...

THAT'S IT! WE'RE SAFE NOW...

UH, HUH. YES, ONCE AGAIN YOU CERTAINLY HAD THINGS COMPLETELY UNDER CONTROL THE WHOLE TIME...

SO, CAN YOU TELL ME WHAT WE DO NOW?

WELL...

SILLY QUESTION! CRRR... WE'RE GO DO THE MASTE IN, AREN'T WE LAURELINE? CHEC OUT...

ALL WE HAVE TO DO IS FOLLOW THE KLAAR, AND... CRITCH... WE'LL REACH HIM. THEN... CRUCK... WE'LL BE FREE AND I'LL SEE MANADIL AGAIN.

YOU'RE PROBABLY RIGHT, SÜL. BESIDES, IT'S THE ONLY THING LEFT TO DO...

AH! I KNEW YOU'D HEAR THE CALL OF DUTY AGAIN...

DUTY... PFFT. I'M DOING IT FOR SÜL, NOT FOR DUTY.

DUTY? WHAT'S THAT?... ANOTHER ONE OF THOSE MOLECULE-BUSTING IDEAS, I'M SURE...

I'M TELLING YOU... BLOOK... OUR ONLY DUTY IS PROSPECTING, THAT'S ALL!

OBJECTIVELY SPEAKING, DUTY IS THE EXPRESSION OF SOCIAL FORCES...

I BEG TO... PLUTSH... DIFFER! IT'S A SUBJECTIVE NOTION THAT...

I'M GOING FLY... CLICK. LITTLE FOR PEOPLE!

MAYBE WE SHOULD... CRRAAA... CHANGE OUR OUTFITS TO VISIT THIS MASTER...

AND DO SOMETHING FOR OUR ORGANISER. I FIND THAT GIRL SIMPLY TOO UNKEMPT...

TIME PASSES SLOWLY...

34

ENLY, WHILE THE CHARIOT IS
SING A WIDE PLATEAU COVERED
A FOUL-SMELLING FILM OF
KISH WATER...

THE
RDS OF
ADNESS!

I'VE NEVER SEEN SO
MANY!... CRRR... THE
MASTER'S DECIDED TO
GET US THIS TIME!!

THERE!
POSSIBLE
COVER!

THEY'RE
ATTACKING!!

WAC

WE'RE DONE FOR!

NO! COME ON!

THEN, AMIDST THE BIRDS' SHRIEKS AND BEATING WINGS...

EVERYONE AROUND THEM! HURRY!...

... THE BIRDS OF MADNESS CAN'T DO ANYTHING TO US ANYMORE—WE'RE ALL ALREADY MAD!

LET'S SHIELD THEM!

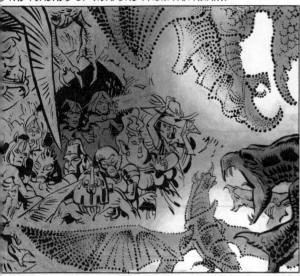

ME, TOO!... PRRR... HORRIBLE SOUNDS!

AAAAH! I'VE BEEN BITTEN!... CRIIITCH... IT'S LIKE STATIC!

HOLD TIGHT! KEEP FIRING!

35 A

THE BIRDS ARE TREATING!

ARE YOU... BZZZ... BADLY HIT?

BAH. I'M USED TO IT BY NOW!... CREEE... I FEEL WEIRD, BUT CONSCIOUS...

VERY INTERESTING... PRRRR... THIS CONFIRMS MY THEORY! THOSE BIRDS... OOG... ARE MERE ILLUSIONS.

SEE!... OOOOP... WE CAN BEAT THE MASTER'S STINKING COPS— AND... CLICK... HIM, TOO, FOR SURE!!

AND THESE BODIES? ILLUSIONS AS WELL? NO, THE YOUNG ONE IS... TAK... RIGHT. THEY'RE THE MASTER'S ENFORCERS.

OK AT US NOW... R... I'M SICK OF SE NASTY BIRDS!

AND I HAVE... BIMP... NOTHING LEFT TO WEAR! THAT HORRIBLE MASTER WILL HEAR ABOUT IT!

HEY! LOOK AT THAT!!

OH, WHAT IS... BIMP... IT THIS TIME?

I'M NOT GOING ANYWHERE... GLUCK... THIS PLACE LOOKS GREAT.

35 B

THIS IS... SCRATCH... A GOOD PLACE TO FLY. SHALL I?!

WHOA! NO CRAZY STUFF... WELL, I MEAN...

HUH?... THERE'S A LIGHT DOWN THERE!?!

AND THERE!! ALL THE PATHS OF THE KLAAR!!!

LET'S GO DOWN

I'M SURE... IKKK... THAT IT'S THE MASTER!

I'VE GOT NOTI AGAINST TH MASTER...

ME, NEITHER! ACTUALLY, I'M GOING TO PROSPECT FOR HIM A BIT...

YOU'RE RIGHT! I'LL GIVE YOU A HAND! WE LAZYBONES CAN BUCKLE DOWN LIKE NO ONE ELSE, YOU'LL SEE!...

HUH?... WHAT ABOUT ME, THEN? THE MASTER AIN'T GONNA LOVE ME IF I DON'T DO ANY WORK...

WHAT DID I TELL YOU?... CLOP... THEY WERE HIT BEFORE US. THE VENOM IS STARTING TO TAKE EFFECT...

NONSENSE. IT'S... PROTCH... THE MASTER'S WILL IMPOSING ITSELF LITTLE BY LITTLE!

AT ANY RATE MIGHT AS W LEAVE THE HERE...

WHAT ABOUT US, VALERIAN?... WE'VE ALL BEEN BITTEN NOW!

YES, WE HAVE TO HURRY.

WE'D DAMNED WELL BETTER... BECAUSE I HAVE NO INTENTION... SLUP... OF SPENDING THE REST OF MY YOUTH SLAVING AWAY FOR THE MASTER!...
**LET'S GO!**

OUGH A STEADILY THICKENING
OSPHERE...

... A DANGEROUS DESCENT BEGINS...

... A FRIGHTENING DIVE INTO
THE MASTER'S IMPREGNABLE
DOMAIN...

... UNTIL, AT LAST...

THE MASTER!

I CAN'T BELIEVE MY EYES!!

I CAN, O[F] COURSE... IKKK... B[UT] WHAT CAN [I] DO AGAINS[T] THAT THING[?]

PROTEST POLITELY...

... BUT FIRMLY!

DO IT IN... SCREEE... I TELL YOU!

ANALYSE THE PRODUCTION PROCESS THAT'S THE FOUNDATION OF ITS POWER AND DEMONSTRATE TO IT THAT...

NO, NO! WE NEED TO LOOK DOWN UPON IT UNTIL IT VANISHES OUT OF SHEER MEDIOCRITY!... URG...

THAT'S RIGHT! VEX IT BY FLYING HIGHER THAN... BRINK... ITS LOUSY BIRDS!

FORCE IT TO LEAVE! THAT'S... CLICK... WHAT WE NEED TO DO!

THE KLAAR INFLOWS! IF WE REMOVE THEM... GRRR... WE STARVE IT OUT. AND IF WE STARVE IT OUT...

GOT IT! I'LL GIVE IT A SHOT!... GGLLL... TAKE COVER...

ADVANCING SLOWLY ONTO THE OPEN SPACE SURROUNDING THE MASTER...

... TAKE OVER IF I FAIL!

... ITS MASSIVE, SOFT BODY REACTING WITH NOTHING MORE THAN A SLIGHT QUIVERING...

... VALERIAN OPENS FIRE.

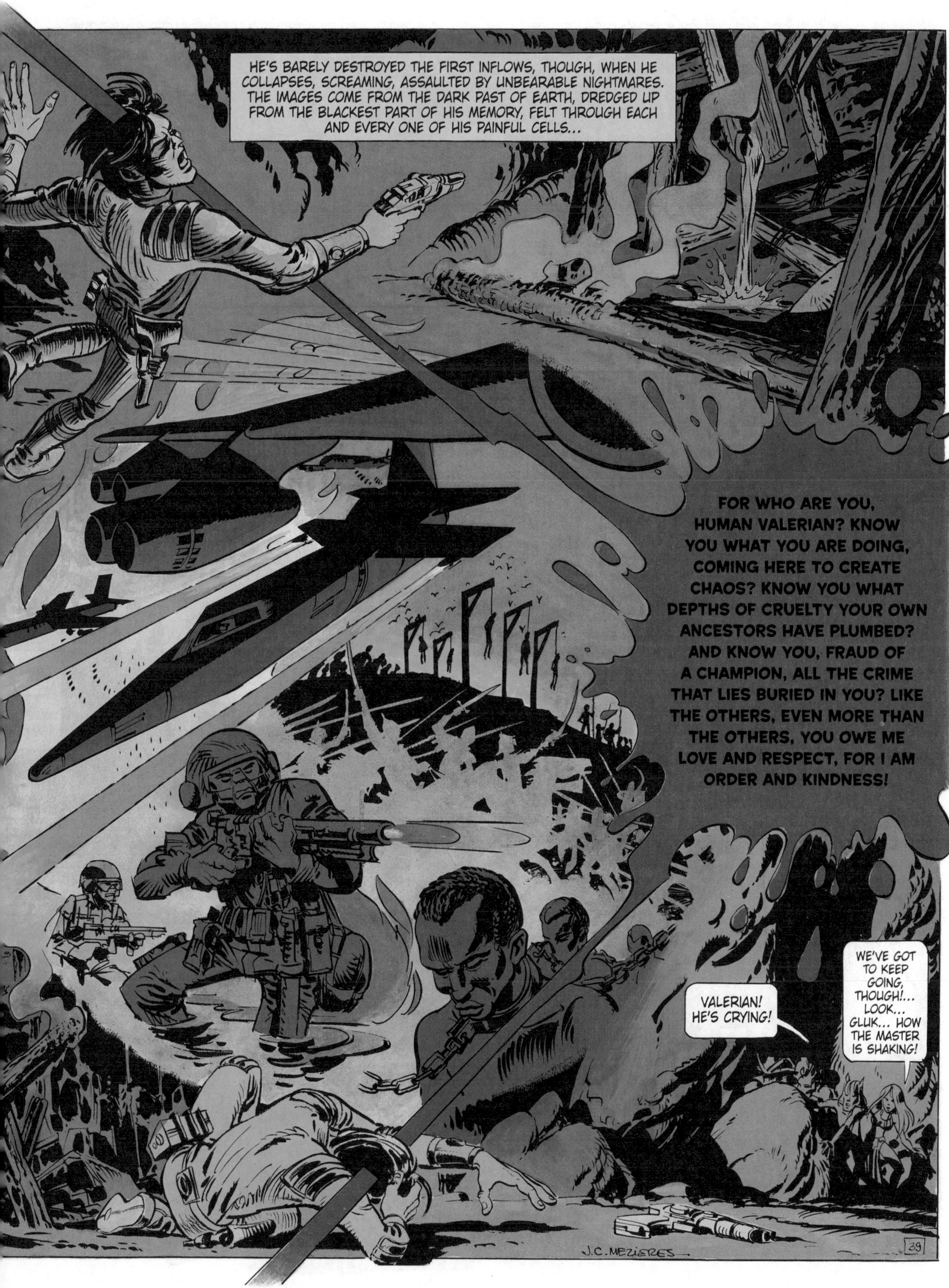
HE'S BARELY DESTROYED THE FIRST INFLOWS, THOUGH, WHEN HE COLLAPSES, SCREAMING, ASSAULTED BY UNBEARABLE NIGHTMARES. THE IMAGES COME FROM THE DARK PAST OF EARTH, DREDGED UP FROM THE BLACKEST PART OF HIS MEMORY, FELT THROUGH EACH AND EVERY ONE OF HIS PAINFUL CELLS...
FOR WHO ARE YOU, HUMAN VALERIAN? KNOW YOU WHAT YOU ARE DOING, COMING HERE TO CREATE CHAOS? KNOW YOU WHAT DEPTHS OF CRUELTY YOUR OWN ANCESTORS HAVE PLUMBED? AND KNOW YOU, FRAUD OF A CHAMPION, ALL THE CRIME THAT LIES BURIED IN YOU? LIKE THE OTHERS, EVEN MORE THAN THE OTHERS, YOU OWE ME LOVE AND RESPECT, FOR I AM ORDER AND KINDNESS!
VALERIAN! HE'S CRYING!
WE'VE GOT TO KEEP GOING, THOUGH!... LOOK... GLUK... HOW THE MASTER IS SHAKING!
J.C. MEZIERES
39

IT'S LAURELINE'S TURN TO LEAP OUT, ONLY TO COLLAPSE SUDDENLY AS WELL, OVERWHELMED BY A THOUSAND EXCRUCIATING VISIONS...

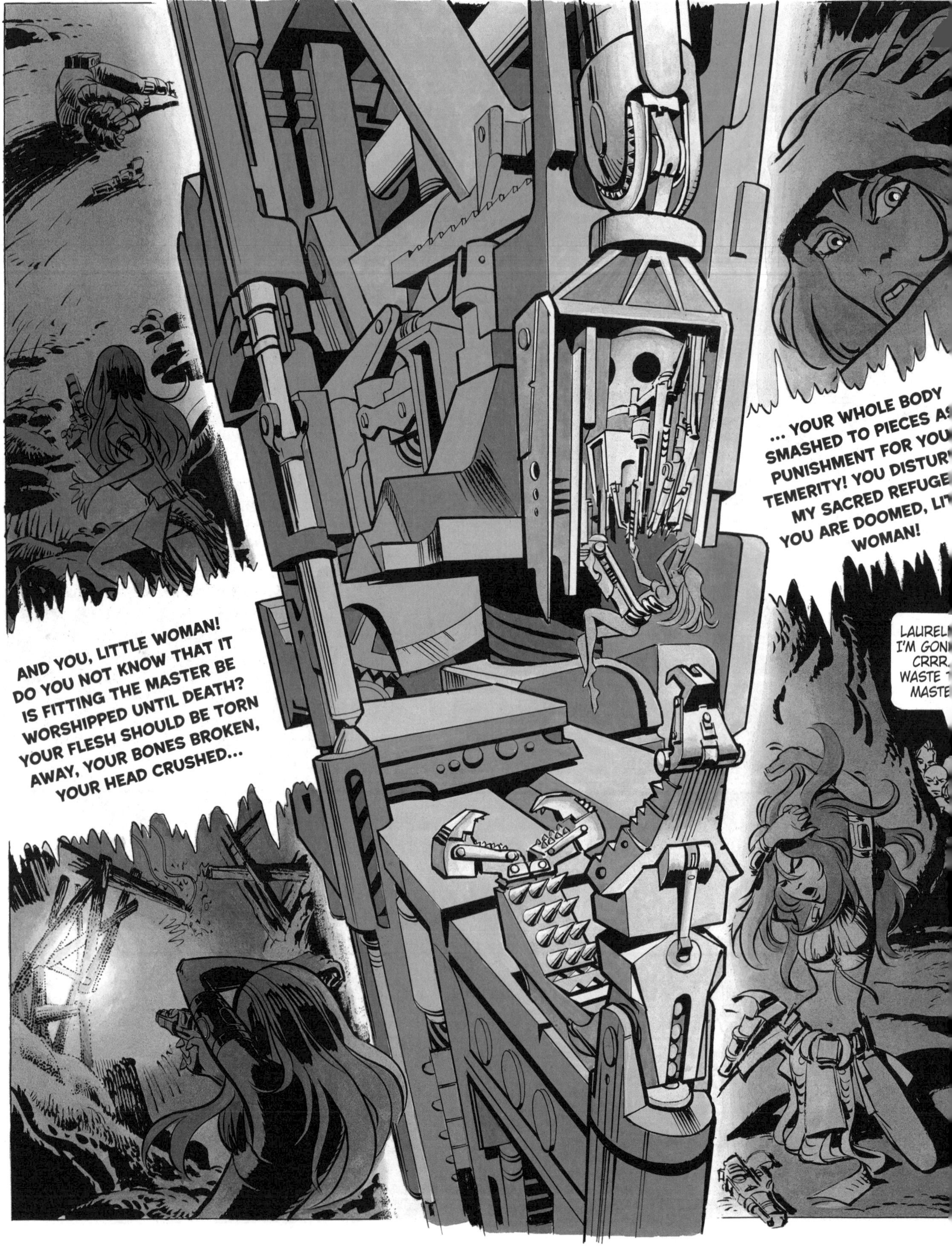
AND YOU, LITTLE WOMAN! DO YOU NOT KNOW THAT IT IS FITTING THE MASTER BE WORSHIPPED UNTIL DEATH? YOUR FLESH SHOULD BE TORN AWAY, YOUR BONES BROKEN, YOUR HEAD CRUSHED...
... YOUR WHOLE BODY SMASHED TO PIECES AS PUNISHMENT FOR YOU TEMERITY! YOU DISTUR MY SACRED REFUGE YOU ARE DOOMED, LI WOMAN!
LAUREL I'M GON CRRR. WASTE MASTE

LIKE SÜL, THOUGH, THE MEMBERS OF THE SMALL GROUP COLLAPSE ONE BY ONE. SOON, A SCENE OF LITTER DESOLATION UNFOLDS OVER THE KLAAR SPILLING TO THE GROUND WITH A WARM FRAGRANCE—ANOTHER TORTURE TO THE STARVING BAND—AS ALL OF THEM GIVE IN TO THEIR OWN NIGHTMARES AND TERRORS...

-EATING SPONGES FOR THOSE HAILING
M DISTANT ERISTRENE...

... FOUL, SLIMY GLATUFILS THAT THE CHILDREN OF RUMUL FEAR SO MUCH...

... VENOMOUS STONES THAT TERRIFY THE INHABITANTS OF ORTOKZOK.

AND YET...

DREAMS—IT'S ALL JUST DREAMS! I... ARRGH... KNOW IT...

WE ARE NO CLACK... GO TO FEEL SOF FOR OURSEL

HEY!... VALERIAN! CAN YOU HEAR ME?

YES... OHHH... URG... MY HEAD!!

THE MASTER... HE'S DESTROYING... GRRNN... US BECAUSE WE'RE ATTACKING HIM SEPARATELY. ALL TOGETHER... LIKE WE DID WITH THE BIRDS... WE CAN WIN...

YES... GET... EVERYONE UP...

HOLD ME TIGHT!

I'M HERE!

TAKE MY HAND!

VALERIAN, HELP ME...

LOOK UPON THE MASTER!

44

AND SUDDENLY, WITH A GREAT TEARING SOUND...

SEE HOW HE QUAKES!

BRAOOM

THE MASTER HAS FLED!!

HE TOOK THAT HORRIBLE MIST WITH HIM!

UP THERE! THE FEW REMAINING BIRDS ARE FOLLOWING IT!

FINALLY—I CAN'T HEAR THOSE HORRIBLE NOISES ANYMORE!

NO MORE MASTER!

AH! I'VE BEEN HUNGRY FOR SO LONG. LET'S CELEBRATE!

PURE NECTAR!! YOU KNOW... THIS CRUISE MAKES ME WANT TO...

...STAY HERE, AFTER ALL? THE ATMOSPHERE IS IMPROVING!

MAYBE ONCE I'M WELL FED, I CAN ACTUALLY FLY FOR REAL!

NOT AT ALL! THE BEAUTY OF SEIZING POWER IS THE VICTORY OVER A CLASS ENEMY... 'SCUSE ME, MOVE OVER A BIT...

MMM... THIS LIQUID IS DELICIOUS! IT'S AS IF ALL THAT CAME BEFORE NEVER EXISTED, AS IF ALL WAS HARMONY AND BLISS...

HEY, HOW ABOUT WE REBUILD THE KLAAR INFLOWS AND SETTLE DOWN HERE? WOULDN'T THAT BE AWESOME?

YEAH! ROLL ON THE GOOD TIMES!!!

WHOA... DO YOU HEAR THEM?

ERM! SOME REVOLUTION... I'M NOT IMPRESSED!

THIS SEEMS TO ME LIKE THE PERFECT TIME FOR ONE OF THOSE LITTLE SPEECHES YOU LIKE SO MUCH. ONLY, CONVINCING, THIS TIME... YOU KNOW WHAT I MEAN?

HA, HA. VERY FUNNY!

YOU SHOULD BE ASHAMED OF YOURSELVES, THE LOT OF YOU! THE MASTER'S ONLY BEEN GONE A MINUTE AND ALL YOU THINK ABOUT IS TAKING HIS PLACE! WHAT ABOUT ALL THE POOR BASTARDS BREAKING THEIR BACKS UP THERE TO PREPARE THE KLAAR YOU'RE GULPING DOWN? HAVE YOU THOUGHT ABOUT THEM, HUH?!

HEY, SOUNDS LIKE HE'S BETTER THAN USUAL. IT'S SOLID SNAPPY... FINALLY.

ND YOU, SÜL? DON'T U WANT TO SEE YOUR BEAUTIFUL PLANET AGAIN?

WELL... YEAH...

SO?

YES... WE WERE RATHER SILLY, WEREN'T WE?

MAYBE WE DID LOSE CONTROL A LITTLE...

BUT IT'S OVER NOW. WE'RE LEAVING!

ER... MY FEET LEFT THE GROUND FOR A MOMENT...

IT'S JUST THAT WE HAVEN'T HAD MUCH CHANCE TO HAVE FUN UNTIL NOW...

THAT KLAAR GOES RIGHT TO YOUR HEAD!

LET'S GO, THEN! WE'LL TELL THE MASTER'S CITIES AND LANDS THAT THEY'RE FREE!

I GUESS THIS MISSION IS A COMPLETE AND RESOUNDING SUCCESS, THEN. RIGHT, O MIGHTY LEADER?

45A

R, IN THE MIDDLE OF STARSHIP CEMETERY...

THAT'S IT! THEY'RE FREE!

45B

... THEN, ABOVE THE SMALL PLANETOID STILL LOCKED ON ITS ERRATIC COURSE...

WELL! THE LIFT-OFF WENT MUCH BETTER THAN THE LANDING!

YES. BUT THE SHIP NEEDS A FULL CHECK-UP AS SOON AS WE REACH GALAXITY. HALF THE INSTRUMENTS ARE DEAD.

BETTER MAKE IT QUICK, THEN, BECAUSE I REALLY MISS MANADIL!

... THROUGH THE DARK DEPTHS OF SPACE...

DON'T WORRY, SÜL. SINCE YOU'RE THE ONLY ONE WHO DECIDED TO LEAVE THE MASTER'S FORMER DOMINIONS, YOU'LL SOON BE BACK HOME.

DO YOU THI THE OTHER WILL MAKE DOWN THER

... WHERE ENCOUNTERS WITH UNKNOWN LIFE FORMS STILL FILL MAN WITH TERROR...

HMM... IT WON'T BE EASY FOR THEM TO LEARN TO BE FREE AGAIN. BUT THEY DESTROYED THE KLAAR BASINS AND ARE REORGANISING THEIR PRODUCTION ALONG A COMMUNAL BASIS, SO IT'S OFF TO A GOOD START... IT'LL BE UP TO THEM!

... WHERE THE MYSTERY OF THE UNSPEAKABLE IS STILL PRESENT...

I'M MORE WORRIED ABOUT THE FACT THAT THE MASTER IS SOMEWHERE OUT THERE...

YES. AND, SINCE HIS POW COMES FROM OTHERS RESIGNATION, HE WON HAVE ANY TROUBLE FIND PLACES WHERE THEY L AUTHORITY! HE'S A CUNN ONE, THAT BIG GLUTTO

... WHERE EVERYTHING IS POSSIBLE, THE SHIP FLIES AWAY...

WELL, LET'S JUST HOPE HE KEEPS TO LESS FREQUENTED AREAS...

SO, ARE WE JUMPING TO YOUR GALAXY OR WHAT?

YES, WE'RE READY.

THE END

SCRIPT: CHRISTIN
DRAWING: J.C. MEZIERE 1973